Cool
Slumber Parties

Perfect Party Planning for Kids

Karen Latchana Kenney

A Division of ABDO

ABDO
Publishing Company

visit us at www.abdopublishing.com

Published by ABDO Publishing Company, a division of ABDO, P.O. Box 398166, Minneapolis, Minnesota 55439. Copyright © 2012 by Abdo Consulting Group, Inc. International copyrights reserved in all countries. No part of this book may be reproduced in any form without written permission from the publisher. Checkerboard Library™ is a trademark and logo of ABDO Publishing Company.

Printed in the United States of America, North Mankato, Minnesota
052011
092011

 PRINTED ON RECYCLED PAPER

Interior Design and Production: Colleen Dolphin, Mighty Media, Inc.
Cover Design: Aaron DeYoe
Series Editor: Liz Salzmann
Photo Credits: Colleen Dolphin, Shutterstock

The following manufacturers/names appearing in this book are trademarks:
Darice® Stretchy Cord, DMC Creative World® Embroidery Needles, Office Depot® Poster Board, Old Home® Plain Yogurt, Quaker® Oats, Reynolds® Cut-Rite® Wax Paper

Library of Congress Cataloging-in-Publication Data

Kenney, Karen Latchana.
  Cool slumber parties : perfect party planning for kids / Karen Latchana Kenney.
      p. cm. -- (Cool parties)
  Includes index.
  ISBN 978-1-61714-976-4
  1. Children's parties--Juvenile literature. 2. Sleepovers--Juvenile literature. I. Title.
  GV1205.K47 2012
  793.2'1--dc22
                            2011004213

Contents

It's Slumber Party Time!

You get to have a slumber party! Can you believe it? Your friends can come over and stay the night. You'll eat great food and play fun games. You can even make a craft or two. It will be a blast!

But to make this party happen, you need to plan out the **details**. Start with the basics, like the *when* and *where* of the party. Then move on to details like decorations and **menus**. Create some cool invitations and send them out. And don't forget to plan the activities! They keep the party moving at a fun pace.

Remember to plan and do as much as you can before the party starts. It takes time and hard work to be a host. But it's definitely worth it! Then all that's left for you to do is have fun!

Safety

◎ Ask for an adult's help when making food for your party.

◎ Find out where you can make crafts and play games. Do you need to protect a table surface? What should you use?

◎ Check the party room. Can anything be broken easily? Ask a parent to remove it before the party.

Permission

◎ Where in the house can you have the party? Are any rooms off-limits?

◎ How much money can you spend? Where can you shop and who will take you?

◎ Make sure guests' parents know who will be overseeing the party.

◎ Can you put up decorations? How?

◎ How late can you stay up? What time should the party end the next day?

◎ Talk about who will clean up after the party.

Party Planning Basics

Every great party has the same basic **details**. They are the *who, what, when,* and *where* of the party. Your party planning should begin with these basics. Then make lists of everything you need to buy, make, and do for the party. You should also have a list of everyone you invited. Mark whether each guest can come or not.

Who: How many friends do you want to invite? And who will they be? Try to pick friends who will get along and have fun.

What: What is the theme party for? Is it your birthday? Or just for fun? You'll need to explain this on the invitation.

When: Parties are best on the weekends. Pick a Saturday or Sunday. But don't plan the party on a weekend with a holiday.

Where: Is the party at your house, at a park, or at a party room? Explain the details to your guests. And don't forget to include directions!

Favors:

What to buy:

What to make:

Activities:

What to buy:

What to make:

Menu:

Decorations:

What to buy:

What to make:

Music:

Equipment:

Guests:

_____ yes/no

_____ yes/no

_____ yes/no

_____ yes/no

_____ yes/no

_____ yes/no

What's Your Theme?

It's fun to have a theme for your party. A theme party has a central idea or style. Playing board games is a great theme. Or how about a camping theme? It can be fun inside or outside!

There are so many themes to choose from. Pick one that's fun. Then plan all the **details** around that theme. For example, you can make up your own game for a games party. Or make s'mores at a camping party. Using a theme makes all the elements of your party go together. Check out the party themes on the next page. There are activities in this book to match each one.

Spa

A spa party is all about **pampering** yourself. Apply face masks and paint your nails. And then just relax!

Swimming

Jump in the water and hang out on the beach or by the pool. A swimming party is perfect on a hot day.

Games

Have fun with your friends at a game party. Play your favorite games, or learn some new ones. Try making up your own game!

Camping

Set tents up in your yard or in your living room. Either way, a camping party is fun. It's all about nature.

Glam

Get fancy with a **glam** party. Dress up, wear jewelry, and eat tiny finger foods. Get ready to sparkle at this party!

Art

Do you like to be creative? You can make great art projects at an art party. Make things with paper, beads, **fabric**, or clay. Crafts are even more fun with your friends!

Style Switch-Up

Clean out your closet. Then bring your old clothes to a style switch-up party. Switch with your friends. See what fresh, new styles you'll find!

Don't forget...

After you pick your theme, let guests know all about it. Do they need to bring something or wear special clothes? Let them know on the invitation. That way guests will show up prepared. They'll also be even more excited to party!

Tools & Supplies

Here are some of the things you'll need to do the activities in this book:

butter

mixing bowls

oats

marshmallows, large

plain yogurt

cucumber slices

milk chocolate bar

paper plate

washcloth

graham crackers

measuring cups

rolling pin

honey

wax paper

cookie sheet

blender

card stock

⅛-inch hole punch

tape measure

posterboard

string

markers

wooden discs

old sweater

face lotion

ribbon

beads

plastic zipper bag, large

seam ripper

thread

fabric scraps

silk beading cord

needle

pins

colored paper key tags

11

Wrist Twist Invitation

Just twist your wrist to read the details!

What You Need

paper
pen
colored paper key tags
⅛-inch hole punch

ArtTheme

1. Break your party **details** into five or six parts. Each part should be only a few words. For example, the parts could be "Slumber," "Party!" "Laura's House," "Aug. 11," "5:00 p.m.," and "bring sleeping bag." Write them down on a sheet of paper so you don't forget.

2. Choose six key tags. Punch a hole in each one. Put the hole opposite the hole with the key ring.

3. Lay the tags down. They should all face the same way. Write one of the party detail parts on each tag. Write small and neatly.

4. Connect the tags by putting the key ring of one tag through the hole you punched in the next tag. Make sure the tags are in the right order!

5. Send them to your friends. They will love wearing these cool invitations!

More Ideas!

CAMPING THEME
Make night scene invitations. Use black paper as the background. Glue silver glitter at the top. Cut a tent shape out of white paper. Write the party details on it. Glue it to the card.

STYLE SWITCH-UP THEME
Make paper doll invitations with scrapbook paper dresses. Write the details on the dresses. Make each one different and fun! The party details should be the same though!

SWIMMING THEME
Make invitations shaped like flip-flops. Cut paper in the shape of a flip-flop sole. Write the party details on it. Add **straps** made of paper or ribbon.

Beach Ball Banner

String it up and see how cheerful it looks!

What You Need

thin paper plates
pencil
markers
hole punch
string, 6 feet (2 m)
tape

Swimming Theme

1 Use a pencil to draw the sections of a beach ball on six paper plates. Put a small circle near the top. Then draw four curved lines from the circle to the bottom.

2 Color the beach balls with markers. Use a lot of bright colors. Make each one a little different.

3 Spell "PARTY!" on the plates with black marker. Write one letter on each plate. Put the exclamation point on the sixth plate.

4 Punch two holes near the top of each plate. Put one on each side of the top circle.

5 Thread the string through the holes in the plates. Space the plates evenly. Tape the string to the backs of the plates so they don't slide around. Tie or tape the ends of the string to a wall or fence.

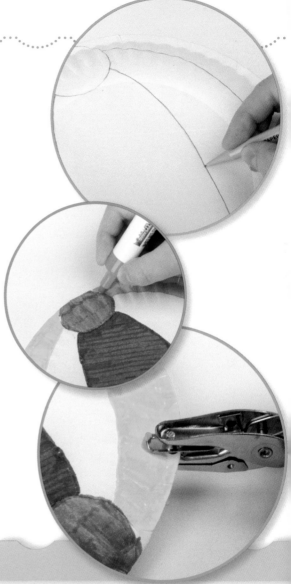

More Ideas!

CAMPING THEME
Cut stars out of posterboard. Paint them with glow-in-the dark paint. Punch holes in them and hang them up with string. Use flashlights for nighttime fun.

SPA THEME
Arrange clean washcloths in a basket. Put new, pretty hair ties out in a glass bowl. Lie on fluffy pillows on the floor and play relaxing music.

GAMES THEME
Make a cool dice decoration for the table. Paint two square boxes to look like giant dice. Then set them on a checkered tablecloth.

15

Fun & Fab Jewels

What You Need

ribbon
silk beading cord
tape measure
scissors
large beads

These jewels are fabulous at the party and after!

Glam Theme

1. Cut four 8-inch (20 cm) pieces of ribbon. Cut a piece of cord that is 18 inches (46 cm) long.

2. Lay the ribbons on top of each other. Tie one end of the cord around the middle of the ribbons. Leave about 3 inches (8 cm) of cord on one side.

3. Put a bead on the longer side of the cord. Tie a knot as close to the bead as possible.

4. Add more beads, knotting the cord after each bead.

5. Test the length after you have about 5 inches (13 cm) of beads. Wrap it around your wrist and hold the ends together. Do the beads go all the way around your wrist? Can you fit your hand through to take it off?

6. Stop adding beads when it is the right length. Tie the ends of the cord together. Tie it so the last bead is right next to the ribbons. Cut off any extra cord.

More Ideas!

GAMES THEME
Make travel tic-tac-toe games. Use an empty metal candy tin. Make the board on the top with thin strips of black duct tape. Put button magnets inside the tin for the game pieces.

SPA THEME
Make **cozy** spa slippers for your friends. Cut two foot shapes out of thin foam. Slip each one into the bottom of a clean sock. Write your friends' names with puffy paint on the soles.

STYLE SWITCH-UP THEME
Give out little sewing kits. Your friends can use them to fix or alter their new clothes. Include cool patches and fancy buttons.

What's on the Menu?

A great party isn't complete without delicious snacks and cool drinks! It's best to make finger foods. They are fun to eat and easy to carry. Everyone can still mingle while they snack. To plan your party **menu**, think about a few things first.

Variety

Everyone has different tastes. Make sure you have some sweet and some salty things. Have healthy choices and **vegetarian** dishes too.

Meals

Slumber parties last a long time. You will probably need more than just snacks. Are your guests coming early enough for dinner? Will you offer breakfast in the morning before they leave? And maybe they'll want snacks too!

Amount

How many people are coming? Plan to have enough food to feed everyone.

Time

It takes time to shop for and prepare food. Pick recipes that you have time to make. Remember, there are other things you need to do before the party.

Allergies

Check with your guests to see if they have any food **allergies**. Make sure there are things those guests can eat.

Sample Party Menus

It's fun to plan your menu around your party theme. Here are some examples.

Simply Spa Menu

Fresh Fruit Kebabs

Salad Cups

Mini Turkey Wraps

Sparkling Water with Lime Wedges

Blueberry Smoothies

Cool Camping Menu

Banana Boats

Hearty Hamburger with Cheese

Foil Baked Potato

Inside-Out S'mores*
*recipe on page 22!

Ginger Ale Punch

Oh-So-Glam Menu

Cheese Puffs

Artichoke Dip on Mini-Toasts

Chocolate Fondue

Strawberry Cupcakes with Sprinkles

Sparkling Punch

That's So Artsy Menu

Stained Glass Cookies

Veggie Bouquet

Palette of Dips

Masterpiece Mini Pizzas

Rainbow Slushies

Ask for help finding easy and delicious recipes to make.

Inside-Out S'mores

Serve no-fire fancy s'mores at your party!

CampingTheme

1   Line the cookie sheet with wax paper. Put 8 to 10 graham crackers in the plastic bag. Crush the crackers with the rolling pin. Then pour the crumbs into a bowl.

2   Put the chocolate bar and the butter in a bowl. Microwave for 1 minute and then stir. Keep repeating until the chocolate is melted and smooth. It should look like chocolate syrup.

3   Dip each marshmallow halfway into the chocolate.

4   Then gently press them onto the graham cracker crumbs.

5   Place the marshmallows on the wax paper. When the cookie sheet is full, put it in the refrigerator to chill for 20 minutes.

6   To serve, arrange the inside-out s'mores on a large plate.

Don't Forget Breakfast!

End your slumber party with a good breakfast in the morning. Here are a couple of delicious ideas.

Layer yogurt and fresh fruit in fancy glasses. Sprinkle granola and berries on top.

Serve different kinds of bagels. Make flavored spreads by mixing jam or seasonings into plain cream cheese.

Funky Arm Warmers

Switch up your style by recycling a sweater!

24

Style Switch-Up Theme

1. Practice the blanket **stitch** on a **fabric** scrap. Thread the needle and tie a knot at one end of the thread. Start at the back of the fabric and push the needle to the front. Do this again but do not pull the thread tight. Put the needle through the **loop**. Then pull the thread tight. Repeat this stitch along the edge of the fabric. When finished, tie the loose thread to the last stitch.

2. Cut the sleeves off the sweater. Try to make them the same length.

3. Make thumb holes about 1 to 2 inches (3 to 5 cm) from the ends of the sleeves. Use the seam ripper to make a 1-inch (3 cm) hole in each sleeve's seam.

4. Now it's time to use the blanket stitch! Stitch around each thumb hole. Fold the cut ends of the sleeves to the inside. Pin the folds in place. Then use the blanket stitch again to finish the edges.

5. Remove the pins and try on your restyled arm warmers!

More Ideas!

SWIMMING THEME
It's fun to make plain flip-flops show your style. Glue decorative gems to the **straps** or add a silk flower. You could also tie on pretty ribbons.

GAMES THEME
Make your own dice out of clay. Use fun colors, not just plain black and white. Make the cubes one color. Use another color for the dots.

ART THEME
Create cool paper art using patterned paper. Fold **origami** paper into animals. Or cut out shapes and make one-of-a-kind collages.

25

Soothing Face Mask

This mask makes your skin feel super soft!

What You Need

measuring cups
⅔ cup oats
blender
½ cup plain yogurt
¼ cup honey
mixing bowl
spoon
hair tie
cucumber slices
washcloth
face lotion

Spa Theme

This recipe makes a mask for one person.

1 Put the oats in the blender. Put the cover on and grind the oats into powder.

2 Put the yogurt and honey in the mixing bowl and add the oats. Mix into a paste.

3 Tie your hair back away from your face. Then use your fingertips to apply the mask. But don't put any near your eyes!

4 Sit back and put cucumber **slices** over your eyes. Then just relax!

5 After 15 minutes, remove the mask. Use a wet washcloth to gently wipe it off. Then smooth on face lotion. Doesn't your skin shine?

More Ideas!

STYLE SWITCH-UP THEME
After you've switched clothes, have a fashion show! Make interesting outfits using the swapped clothes. Then show off your new style.

GLAM THEME
Make even your nails look **glamorous**! Paint flowers and **designs** on them with nail art pens. Add nail jewels or glitter to the wet paint for extra sparkle!

ART THEME
Make colorful braided friendship bracelets. Tie beads to the ends of the strings. Exchange bracelets with your friends.

Fun Friend Trivia

What You Need

- posterboard
- pencil
- markers
- wooden discs
- card stock, cut into squares
- scissors

How much do you know about your friends?

START

Games Theme

1. Before the party, make a game board on the posterboard. Draw a winding path. Write "start" at one end and "finish" at the other end. Divide the path into squares. Color the squares using five different colors.

2. Color wooden discs to use as game pieces. Make each one different.

3. Ask each of your friends to think of ten questions about himself or herself. For example, Who has a pet lizard named Harry?

4. Have your friends write their questions and answers on the square cards. Then write one of the path colors on each card.

5. To play the game, have the first person draw a card and read the question. The person next in the circle answers. If the answer is right, the person moves his or her piece to the next square that is the color written on the card. Keep going around the circle. The first person to reach the finish wins!

More Ideas!

GLAM THEME
Play star-studded **charades**. Set up a stage and a spotlight. Then watch guests pretend to be famous actors and actresses. See who can guess who they are.

SWIMMING THEME
Splash tag is a great game for a hot day. Give everyone a big, soft sponge. Get them wet. Then tag each other by swinging the sponges so the water flies off.

CAMPING THEME
Hold a nature scavenger hunt. You could do it in your yard or go to a park. Give each guest a list of things to find. See who finds everything first.

Conclusion

What a great slumber party! Everyone had a fun time. And many new memories were made. But, the party room is a mess! There's still work to do. Make sure you clean up and put everything back in order. Your parents will see what a responsible party host you are.

Was it your birthday? Did you keep track of your gifts? It's important to write down who gave you what. That will make sending thank-you cards easier. Make thank-you cards that match the party's theme. Write something **unique** and personal on each guest's card. It will make your friends feel special. Then send out the cards within a week after the party.

Hosting a party is hard work! There are so many **details** to plan and things to make. In the end, though, it all comes together to make a party to remember! Slumber parties are so much fun, but what will your next party be? Check out the other books in the *Cool Parties* series for great ideas.

Glossary

allergy – sickness caused by touching, breathing, or eating certain things.

charades – a game in which one person acts something out, and the others have to guess what it is.

cozy – warm and comfortable.

design – a decorative pattern or arrangement.

detail – a small part of something.

fabric – woven material or cloth.

glamorous – beautiful and exciting. *Glam* is short for glamorous.

loop – a circle made by a rope, string, or thread.

menu – a list of things to choose from.

origami – the Japanese art of folding paper into shapes.

pamper – to treat yourself or someone else in a special way.

slice – a thin piece cut from something.

stitch – a small length of thread left in fabric by moving the needle in and out one time.

strap – a strip of leather, cloth, or plastic that holds a shoe on a foot.

unique – different, unusual, or special.

vegetarian – without any meat.

Web Sites

To learn more about cool parties, visit ABDO Publishing Company on the World Wide Web at **www.abdopublishing.com**. Web sites about cool parties are featured on our book links page. These links are routinely monitored and updated to provide the most current information available.

Index